**Br** eaking
**Ba** d

# 30 WAYS TO COOK CHICKEN

ROCKPOINT

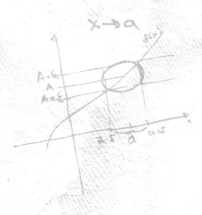

30 Ways to Cook Chicken
Published by Rock Point
Copyright © Frances Lincoln Limited 2015

Designed by Sarah Allberrey

Rock Point is an imprint of the Quarto Publishing Group USA, Inc.
276 Fifth Avenue, Suite 206
New York, New York 10001

ISBN: 978-1-63106-136-3
Printed in China

2 4 6 8 10 9 7 5 3 1

# CONTENTS

# 1. Roas Ted

salt

## Ingredients:

- One oven-ready chicken, weighing about 3lb 5oz / 1.5kg
- Butter
- Salt & pepper

Preheat your oven to 190ºC/375ºF/gas 5. Place your chicken in a roasting dish and smother it in butter. Season with salt and pepper and wrap in kitchen foil. Cook in the centre of the oven for around 1 hour and 20 minutes, removing the foil towards the end so that the skin gets nice and crispy. To check that the chicken is ready, pierce the thigh with a skewer and if the juices run clear, you're good to go!

roast chicken

# 2. In a $S$andwich

## ...with pesto

### Ingredients:

- Two slices of your preferred bread
- Butter (optional)
- Cold chicken
- Pesto of your choice
- Salad of your choice
- Salt & pepper

---

Butter your bread if you are that way inclined and then place your required amount of chicken on one of the slices.

Drizzle, dollop or smother your chosen pesto onto the chicken, add the salad ingredients, season to taste and cover with the second slice of bread. Don't forget to cut the crusts off!

chicken sandwich

# 3. On a SK¹⁹ewer

**SERVES 4**

## ...with satay sauce

### Ingredients:

- 500g/1lb Chicken cubes (marinated in soy, honey, garlic and ginger if you like)
- 150g/5oz peanut butter
- Crushed garlic to taste
- Chilli flakes to taste

- Grated ginger to taste
- 1 tbsp of honey
- Oil – just a dash
- 150 ml coconut oil
- Juice of 1 lime

Blitz together the peanut butter, garlic, ginger, chilli flakes, honey and oil adding more ingredients to taste as you go along; you're the alchemist here. When you're happy with your concoction, add the coconut milk and lime, also to taste.

Put your chicken cubes on skewers and fry them on a high heat until they are cooked through, you'll need to keep turning them.

Serve with the satay sauce.

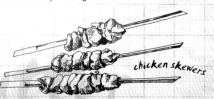

*chicken skewers*

# 4. On a $\boxed{\overset{15}{P}}$izza

## ...with chorizo

## Ingredients:

*Measures depend on the size of your pizza base and your appetite.*

- One pizza base
- Tomato sauce
- Cooked chicken
- Sliced chorizo
- Green peppers or a vegetable of your choice
- Mozzarella or a cheese of your choice

Preheat the oven to 220ºC/425ºF/gas 7.

Spread your pizza base with tomato sauce and add the ingredients in any way you want. Cook for around 10 minutes; you'll know when it's ready.

$3x^2 + 3x \times h + h^2 =$

pizza

# 5. With Pe**As** [33]

## ...in a curry

**SERVES 4**

chilli

### Ingredients:

- 200g/7oz of diced chicken
- 140g/5oz of peas
- 140g/5oz of water
- 1 onion, chopped
- 1 tsp curry powder

- 1 tbsp oil
- 1 tsp turmeric
- 1 clove garlic, crushed
- Chilli powder or fresh chilli to taste

Fry the onion and garlic in the oil until soft. Add the diced chicken and cook until browned. Add the turmeric, chilli and curry powder and stir for a minute or two to coat the chicken in the spices. Add the water and peas then reduce the heat under the pan and simmer for at least 10 minutes, but if you're not in a hurry simmer for a bit longer. Replace some of the water with coconut milk if you want it a little richer, or add a dash of cream. Season to taste and serve with rice or naan bread.

onion

# 6. In a Stir-Fr[87]y

## SERVES 2    ...with noodles

## Ingredients:

- 4 chicken thighs, chopped into pieces
- 1 red or green pepper or a bit of both if you're feeling adventurous
- Oil for frying
- Garlic to taste, sliced or crushed
- 60g/2oz mangetout or peas
- 2 tbsp soy sauce
- 200ml/7fl oz chicken stock
- Cooked noodles

Heat the oil in a wok and add the chicken and garlic and cook until browned. Add the peppers and cook for a couple of minutes, stirring all the while. Add everything else, reduce the heat slightly and continue to stir for another three or four minutes until the chicken is cooked. Add the noodles and serve.

pepper

chopsticks

soy sauce

# 7. In⁴⁹ a Salad

## ...with orange, watercress and lettuce

### Ingredients:

- Cooked chicken
- Watercress
- Lettuce
- Orange
- Balsamic vinegar
- Olive oil

Shred your cooked chicken and serve it with pieces of orange on a bed of lettuce and watercress leaves dressed with balsamic vinegar and olive oil, mixed and seasoned to taste.

# 8. Wi[Th⁹⁰] Tarragon Sauce

## Ingredients:

**SERVES 4**

- Four chicken breasts
- A good slug of white wine
- 150ml/5 fl oz of chicken stock
- 150ml/5 fl oz of cream
- A bunch of fresh tarragon

white wine

Preheat the oven to 200ºC/400ºF/gas 6.

Fry the chicken breasts skin side down long enough to get the skin brown and then transfer into a roasting dish placing them skin side up and cook for around 20 minutes. Meanwhile, add a good slug of white wine to the leftover juices (but skim off any fat) in the frying pan and reduce down until you have a thick liquid. Add the stock and a couple of sprigs of tarragon and keep it on the heat until the liquid has reduced to two thirds of its original volume. Stir in the cream and bring to the boil before lowering the heat again and letting the sauce reduce a bit more. Remove the sprigs of tarragon and replace with some freshly chopped tarragon to serve, poured over your roasted chicken breasts.

tarragon

# 9. With a Drizzle of HoNey

## ...and a sprinkle of sesame seeds

### Ingredients:

- Cooked chicken
- Toasted sesame seeds
- Honey
- Rice

Griddle, fry or roast your chicken and then drizzle it with honey and sprinkle it with toasted sesame seeds. Serve with rice and vegetables of your choice.

# 10. Hot and S Ti cky

## Ingredients:

- Chicken pieces
- Chilli
- Grated ginger
- Honey
- Oil

ginger

Preheat oven to 180ºC/350ºF/gas 4.

Use an ovenproof frying pan to heat the oil and brown your chicken pieces. Add honey, ginger, chili and seasoning to taste and put the pan in the oven to cook for a further ten minutes or so. Check that the chicken is thoroughly cooked before serving.

chilli

# 11. With $S$ weet and Sour sauce

## Ingredients:

- 175ml/6fl oz chicken stock
- 2 tbsp water
- 2 tbsp corn flour
- 3 tbsp rice wine
- 2 tbsp rice vinegar
- 1 tbsp light brown sugar
- 2 tbsp tomato puree
- 2 tbsp soy sauce

rice wine

Mix all the ingredients and bring to the boil.
Simmer for a few minutes and add salt and
pepper to taste. Serve with chicken and vegetables.

# 12. With Gua**Ca**²⁰mole

$3x^2 + 3 \times h + h^2 = 3x$

## Ingredients:

- Avocado
- Lemon or lime juice
- Garlic
- Onion
- Coriander

*coriander*

Mix it all up to taste; leave it lumpy or mash until smooth. Serve in dollops with salad leaves of your choice and cold chicken.

*lime*

# 13. In a Sandwich

## ...with avocado and bacon

### Ingredients:

- Two slices of your preferred bread
- Butter (optional)
- Cold chicken
- Avocado
- Crispy bacon
- Salt & pepper

avocado

Butter your bread if you like it that way and then place your required amount of chicken, bacon and avocado on to one of the slices. Season to taste and cover with the second slice of bread. Cut the crusts off, if you want!

bread

$$3x^2 + 3 \times h + h^2 = 3x$$

# 14. In a $S^{16}$ tew

## ...with chickpeas

### Ingredients:

- Chicken breast, chopped
- Tinned chickpeas
- Tinned tomatoes
- Onion
- Garlic
- Chicken stock
- Oil
- Herbs of your choice

Heat the oil in a pan and fry the onion and garlic until soft. Add the chicken and cook until browned. Add the remaining ingredients to taste, simmer until cooked. Season and serve with a baked potato or rice.

tomatoes

parsley

# 15. On a Pizza

## ...with pineapple and sweetcorn

### Ingredients:

*Measures depend on the size of your pizza base and your appetite.*

- One pizza base
- Tomato sauce
- Cooked chicken
- Pineapple chunks
- Sweetcorn
- Mozzarella or a cheese of your choice

pineapple

Preheat the oven to 220°C/425°F/gas 7.

Spread your pizza base with tomato sauce and add the ingredients in any way you want. Cook for around 10 minutes; you'll know when it's ready.

pineapple pieces

sweetcorn

# 16. Wrapped in Ba**Co**n

## Ingredients:

- Chicken breasts
- Bacon

peas

---

Preheat the oven to 200°C/400°F/gas 6.

Wrap your chicken breasts in rashers of bacon
or Parma Ham and place them in a roasting dish
to bake in the oven for 20 minutes or until cooked.

Serve with mashed potato and peas if you like.

bacon

# 17. WitH[1] a lime

## ...and coriander dip

### Ingredients:

- 170g/6oz crème fraiche
- Coriander, chopped
- 1 or 2 Limes, juice and zest
- Ginger, grated
- A little bit of sweet chilli sauce

lime

Mix it all together and serve with chicken.

*crème fraiche*

chilli

# 18. With che [Es]⁹⁹ y mashed

## ...butternut squash

garlic

### Ingredients:

- 170g/6oz of butternut squash cut into cubes
- 200ml/7fl oz milk
- 85g/3oz grated cheese
- Garlic

Put the butternut squash, milk and garlic into a saucepan to boil. Reduce the heat and simmer for around 10 minutes, so that the squash becomes tender. Give it a good mash and season with salt and pepper then stir in the grated cheese of your choice.

cheese

# 19. In a sa$\boxed{\text{Nd}}^{60}$ wich

## ...with mozzarella and basil

### Ingredients:

- Two slices of your preferred bread
- Butter (optional)
- Cold chicken
- Mozzarella cheese
- Basil
- Salt & pepper

salt

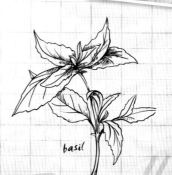

Butter your bread (or brush it with olive oil) and then place your required amount of chicken on one of the slices. Top with sliced mozzarella and basil leaves, drizzle with a little extra-virgin olive oil, season to taste and cover with the second slice of bread.

basil

mozzarella

# 20. With Mango S$\boxed{\text{Al}}^{13}$sa

onion

## Ingredients:

- 1 mango, chopped or sliced
- Lemon juice
- A small amount of finely chopped onion
- Fresh herbs such as mint, basil, coriander

Mix the ingredients together, tasting as you go along.
Serve with chicken, cooked how you like it best.

mango

# 21. In a sa[La]d

## ...with apple, celery and walnuts

### Ingredients:

- Apple, peeled and chopped
- Celery, sliced
- Walnut pieces
- Mayonnaise
- Chicken
- Salad leaves

Combine all the ingredients to make a salad.

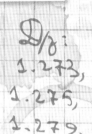

*D/g:*
*1.273,*
*1.275,*
*1.279.*

*salad*

# 22. In⁴⁹ a salad

## ...with chickpeas and feta cheese

### Ingredients:

green pepper

- Cooked chicken
- Tinned chick peas
- Feta cheese, crumbled
- Cucumber chunks
- Green pepper
- Black olives
- Olive oil
- Lemon juice

Mix the ingredients and season with salt and pepper.

cucumber

# 23. In a WRap

## ...with fried zucchini

### Ingredients:

- Cooked chicken
- Fried zucchini sticks
- Chilli jam
- Flat bread

Spread your flat bread with chilli jam to taste. Add the chicken and fried zucchini sticks to the centre of the bread and fold into an easy-to-hold snack.

chicken wraps

# 24. With $\boxed{B^5}$ean Salad

onion

## Ingredients:

- Cooked chicken pieces
- Tinned beans
- Olive oil
- A little thinly sliced red onion
- Lemon zest
- Coriander or any other herb you like

Mix together the beans, herbs, lemon zest and onion leaving the olive oil until last. Place your chicken on a bed of salad leaves and top with the bean salad.

lemon

# 25. With Tomat$O^8$es and Spaghett

$$3x^2 + 3x + 2 + h = 3x$$

## Ingredients:

- Cooked chicken
- Spaghetti
- Cherry tomatoes, halved
- Basil
- Olive oil

- Lemon juice
- Black pepper
- Salt
- Parmesan

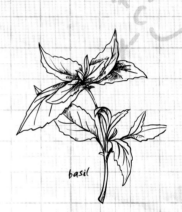

basil

Cook your spaghetti according to the packet instructions and drain, retaining a little of the water. Add the various ingredients to taste with a little bit of the retained water if it seems too dry. Serve it up with a grated parmesan cheese.

spaghetti

# 26. With Rice and RaiSins

## Ingredients:

- Basmati rice
- Sliced chicken breast
- Chopped tomatoes
- Raisins
- Coriander
- Garlic
- Oil
- Salt
- Pepper

Cook the basmati rice according to the packet instructions. Fry the chicken slices with the garlic in the oil adding the raisins and tomatoes. Season to taste and serve on top of the rice with the chopped coriander.

tomatoes

basmati

# 27. In a $\boxed{\overset{16}{\text{S}}}$andwich

## ...with asparagus and parmesan

$$3x^2 + 3 \times h + h^2 = 3x$$

### Ingredients:

- Two slices of your preferred bread
- Butter (optional)
- Cold chicken
- Steamed or griddled asparagus spears
- Parmesan shavings
- Salt & pepper

asparagus

Butter your bread if you like and then place your required amount of chicken, steamed (or griddled) asparagus spears and parmesan shavings on to one of the slices. Season to taste and cover with the second slice of bread.

buttered bread

parmesan

# 28. With MangO [8]

## ...and coconut dip

### Ingredients:

- Coconut milk
- Cream
- Mango
- Salt
- Pepper

Mix some coconut milk with a little dash of cream and some chopped mango, season with salt and pepper and get ready to dip.

salt & pepper

# 29. With Pieapple Salsa

## Ingredients:

- Pineapple
- Roasted red pepper
- Lime, zest and juice
- Chilli

chilli

Cut the pineapple and roasted red pepper into small chunks and mix with the rest of the ingredients to taste.

lime

# 30. As a $\boxed{\overset{73}{\text{Ta}}}$keout

## ...in front of the TV

$$3x^2 + 3x \cdot h + h^2 = 3x$$

tv dinner!

Visit the fast food chicken restaurant of your choice, select your preferred chicken meal, carry home and eat in front of the TV.

$3x^2 + 3x h$

$UeCO_3 \longrightarrow UeO +$

"The finest ingredients are brought together with love and care, then slow cooked to perfection. Yes, the old ways are still best at Los Pollos Hermanos. But don't take my word for it. One taste, and you'll know."

$\dfrac{[H_3O^+] \cdot [S^{2-}]}{[H_2S]}$

$^2 + 3x h + h^2 = 3x$